WORLD'S WORST...

OIL Disasters

Rob Alcraft

HEINEMANN
LIBRARY

First published in Great Britain by Heinemann Library,
Halley Court, Jordan Hill, Oxford OX2 8EJ
a division of Reed Educational and Professional Publishing Ltd.

Heinemann is a registered trademark of Reed Educational & Professional Publishing Ltd.

OXFORD MELBOURNE AUCKLAND
JOHANNESBURG BLANTYRE GABORONE
IBADAN PORTSMOUTH (NH) USA CHICAGO

Designed by Celia Floyd
Illustrations by David Cuzik (Pennant Illustration) and Jeff Edwards
Originated by Dot Gradations, UK
Printed by Wing King Tong, in Hong Kong

04 03 02 01 00
10 9 8 7 6 5 4 3 2 1

ISBN 0 431 01289 X

British Library Cataloguing in Publication Data

Alcraft, Rob, 1966–
    World's worst oil disasters
    1.Oil industries – Accidents – Juvenile literature
    I.Title II.Oil disasters
    363.1'196655

Acknowledgements
The Publishers would like to thank the following for permission to reproduce photographs:
Ann Ronan Picture Library: p.27; Black Star: Charles Mason p.14; Ecoscene: Sally Morgan p.5; Oxford Scientific Films: Michael McKinnon p.20, Richard Packwood p.7; Planet Earth Pictures: Doug Perrine p.25; Rex Features: p.29, ITN p.12, Geoffrey Bollands/Today p.26, Today p.23, P. Nicol p.9; Science Photo Library: Vanessa Vick p.18; Still Pictures: p.19, Bob Evans p.4, Pierre Gleizes p.6, Brent Occlesham p.21, Dominique Halleux p.15; Sygma: S-Compoint p.24.

Cover photograph reproduced with permission of Steve McCurry: Magnum Photos

Our thanks to Dr Henry Wilson of the International Journal of Disaster Prevention and Management, Department of Industrial Technology, University of Bradford for his comments in the preparation of this book.

Every effort has been made to contact copyright holders of any material reproduced in this book. Any omissions will be rectified in subsequent printings if notice is given to the Publisher.

For more information about Heinemann Library books, or to order, please telephone +44 (0)1865 888066, or send a fax to +44 (0)1865 314091. You can visit our web site at www.heinemann.co.uk

Any words appearing in the text in bold, **like this**, are explained in the glossary.

Contents

The Oil Industry

We use oil in everything, from ink to **explosives**. It runs our cars, and fuels our factories. We all depend on it. And because we all need it, oil is very precious. Oil means money, and countries that have a lot of oil are often very rich.

Finding, selling and **refining** oil is one of the world's biggest industries. Companies drill for oil in the frozen lands of Siberia, and in the hot, dry deserts of the Middle East. Amazing technologies have been made that can even pump oil from hundreds of metres below the sea.

An offshore **oil rig** in the Santa Barbara Channel, California, USA.

All over the world governments make laws to prevent accidents and disasters in the oil industry. Companies are expected to make sure that their business is safe and does not pose a threat to people or the **environment**. Yet oil is a world business. Millions of people are involved. Somewhere, sometime, something will always go wrong.

Where does oil come from?

Oil is the remains of tiny plants and animals which lived in the sea millions of years ago. When these living things died, they sank to the bottom. They were covered by mud and sand. Over millions of years weight and heat and tiny **bacteria** changed the animals and plants into oil. Today oil is found in soft spongy rocks, usually trapped deep beneath a layer of hard rock.

Oil for dinner!

When oil comes out of the ground it is thick and usually black. This thick black oil is called crude oil. First it is refined. Refining is a little like cooking, and separates the oil into its many different parts, such as petrol, tar and gas.

These different oil ingredients are made into thousands of different things besides petrol to run cars. For instance, you wear oil in clothes made from nylon, and oil is used in clothes dye. You paint it on your face in make-up. It's used in **fertilizer** for growing food and in medicines to make you better. It's used in car tyres, plastics and **pesticides**. You even eat it, added to your food as colour and **preservative**!

This sticky black substance is crude oil. The world's biggest producer of crude oil is Russia.

When Things Go Wrong

The oil business is dangerous. Oil is often found in places that are difficult to get to, and difficult to work in. There is a constant risk of accidents as people fly to and from **oil rigs**. In deserts where it is very hot, or very cold, machines don't always work well, and people find it hard to concentrate.

Oil burns easily – that's why it is so useful. Also, it often contains, or is found with, gas. A tiny spark can cause fires and explosions. Underground oil is under **pressure** – just like a shaken can of cola. If taps and pipes in **oil wells** crack or burst, oil and gas will roar out. **Capping**, or stopping, an oil well can be difficult and dangerous. In March 1992 oil found in Uzbekistan was under so much pressure that wells drilled into it could not be controlled. The wells broke, and oil gushed hundreds of feet into the air for 62 days.

Following the Gulf War in 1991, whole oil fields were on fire, with billions of gallons of oil blazing out of control.

Oil pollution on a beach in South Devon, England.

Fortunately, many oil spills and fires are small, no-one is killed and the **environment** recovers from the poisonous oil. But sometimes accidents are serious, and there is disaster.

In this book we look at three of the worst disasters to hit the oil business – and the world – this century. We look at the stories of those who were there, and who survived. We look minute by minute at what went wrong and why disaster struck. Is there something about oil that will always spell disaster?

Everyday disaster

Most oil **pollution** isn't caused by single disasters. It is caused by small oil spills and leaks from ships. Around the world two and half times more pollution is caused by ordinary shipping than by dramatic tanker or oil rig accidents. That's why, even if a tanker hasn't run aground on your favourite beach, you may still find patches of thick tarry oil there.

Blow Out!
The Piper Alpha Oil Rig Disaster

Late at night, on 6 July 1988, the Piper Alpha **oil rig** 160km off the east coast of Scotland exploded in flames. 167 men were killed. It was the worst disaster ever to hit the UK oil industry.

Piper Alpha
Scotland
UK

Fireball

The Piper Alpha oil rig was huge. It stood on four giant legs, 92m high, and was home to over 200 workers.

Piper Alpha was used to drill for oil. From deep beneath the seabed the oil was piped to shore. But where there is oil, there is also gas. On Piper Alpha some gas was pumped to land, while some was burnt off in a giant **flare**.

On 4 July men on Piper Alpha say there was a strange smell from the gas on the rig. Something wasn't quite right. Then on 6 July an engineer removed a **valve** in the gas pumping system, so that it could be checked and repaired. Enquiries after the disaster found that he didn't put it back, because the lifting gear he needed was doing other work.

Bill Lobban survived the Piper Alpha disaster. This is his story, which appeared in the *Times* newspaper on 7 July 1988.

There were a lot of flames and smoke and gradually it came into the accommodation section but we managed to find our way out onto the pipe deck.

There were more explosions and the rig tilted to an angle of 30 degrees. It just suddenly dropped down at one side and the explosions continued around us.

It was just terrifying. I ran out when there was a lull in the flames and smoke. We knew this was our one chance. We could touch nothing on deck because it was burning red hot. So we just ran to the edge and jumped straight into the water. Flames were shooting 70 or 100m into the air.

This picture of fire engulfing the Piper Alpha oil rig appeared on the front pages of many newspapers the day after the disaster.

When the shift changed the engineer who had removed the valve went to rest and other men came on duty. It was night and work continued on the floodlit rig. The sea lifted and surged 60m below. Hours went by. Then at 9.45pm the burning gas flare began to roar. Five minutes later a gas pump failed. Gas began to leak, and then **ignited**. Piper Alpha exploded in flames.

Escape from the Inferno

As the Piper Alpha **oil rig** burned there was confusion and shouting. Men climbed out onto the structure of the rig to escape the fire. Some jumped out into the darkness. It was over a 30m jump into freezing seas. It took immense courage.

On the rig itself explosions destroyed fire-fighting equipment. The men on Piper Alpha could do little to fight the fire. They could only try to escape or wait for help. The Piper Alpha rig was burning out of control.

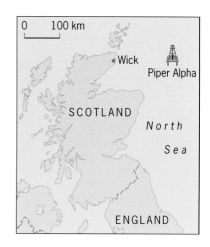

1 At 9.58pm an explosion rips through the Piper Alpha oil rig. Equipment meant to shut down the flow of oil from beneath the sea is blown away. Oil and gas spews into the flames, fuelling the fire, and causing explosion after explosion. Survivors talk of more than 20 explosions.

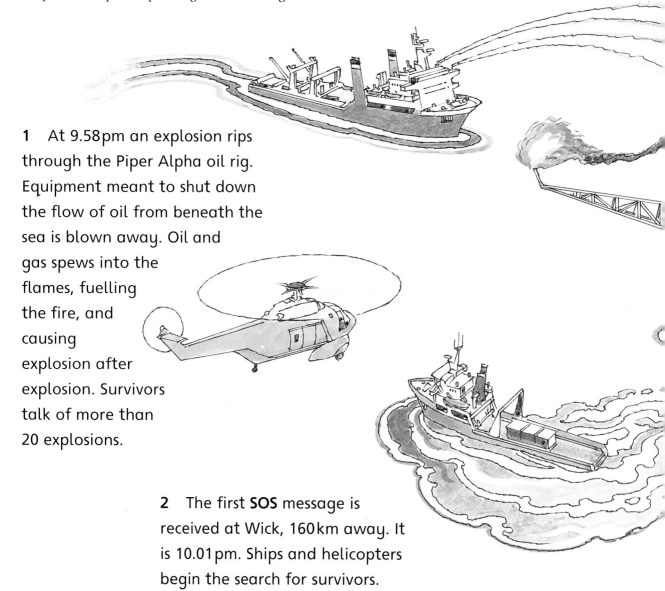

2 The first **SOS** message is received at Wick, 160km away. It is 10.01pm. Ships and helicopters begin the search for survivors.

3   At the time of the first explosion divers are working beneath the rig. As a safety measure automatic fire equipment – supposed to drench the rig with water – has been turned off. There is no way of fighting the fire on Piper Alpha.

4   Men are trapped in the accommodation block. It stands directly above the oil and gas of the main drilling area. The men have been trained to wait for helicopters to **evacuate** them – but the landing pad is destroyed.

5   Beneath the rig a boat called the *Sandhaven* tries to rescue men in the water. But at 10.22pm a second massive explosion engulfs the rig and the ship in a fireball. On the ship three men are killed on deck. A rescue boat is destroyed in the water. Even the sea is burning.

6   The hospital ship *Tharos* treats injured men. Helicopters ferry survivors to the ship and to the shore.

7   By morning little of the rig remains above water. The structure is tilting alarmingly. Oil and gas shoot flames and smoke into the air. A specialist oil fire-fighter, Red Adair, is called in to cap the wells and put out the fires. But bad weather delays action. Six days later two wells on the rig are still burning.

11

The Cold Light of Day

The Piper Alpha oil rig burnt for over a week until fire fighters were able to **cap** the wells.

The Piper Alpha disaster began one of the biggest emergency operations ever in the North Sea. At least 12 ships and six helicopters were sent to help rescuers get men from the **oil rig** and out of the water. By 3am 40 people had been lifted from the sea, but 167 men had died.

How did it happen?

In 1997 a court in Scotland blamed two men – Terence Sutton and Robert Vernon – for causing the disaster. They were the engineers responsible for the missing **valve** in the gas pumping system. But relatives of the men, and oil worker **unions** were angry. The two men had been killed during the disaster, and could not answer the charges. Anyway the evidence was all at the bottom of the sea, so how could anyone really know what had gone wrong? Ann Gillanders, from the Piper Alpha Families and Survivors Association said the court was wrong. She said 'The management was deficient as far as safety was concerned and the buck stops at the top.' She pointed to the long record of fires and accidents on oil rigs in the North Sea. There had been 32 serious accidents on rigs in 1987, and 72 the year before. It was not a good safety record.

Safety experts and many men who had worked on Piper Alpha, said the rig was dangerous. The sleeping accommodation, where 122 men died, was right on top of the most **explosive** and dangerous area on the rig. Safety alarms were also often ignored, and the rig was rusting and unstable. Allan Millar of the Professional Diver Association said: 'That rig [Piper Alpha] had quite a reputation. It was felt that if anything did happen it would be on that particular platform.'

Changes to law

After the disastrous fire on the Piper Alpha oil rig, the British government made changes to some of the safety laws. Today it is law that everyone on an oil platform has a survival suit, life-jacket and other special protective clothing. Everyone on a rig also has to do special training so they know what to do in an emergency. Rigs also have to have quick escape routes to lifeboats.

The Piper Alpha tragedy brought misery to many families.

Wreck!
The Exxon Valdez Oil Disaster

On 25 March 1989 the **supertanker** *Exxon Valdez* smashed into Bligh **Reef** off the Alaskan coast. Its 30,000 tonne cargo of oil spewed into the sea. A deadly 150-km **oil slick** spread from the tanker. It was the worst oil spill in American history.

Alaska

Exxon Valdez oil spill

Heading into disaster

At 9pm the *Exxon Valdez* edged its way from port, and headed out into Alaska's Prince William Sound. The weather was good and the seas calm. At 11.30pm the US Coastguard received a call over the radio. The *Exxon Valdez* wanted permission to steer east, to avoid icebergs up ahead. Permission was given.

The captain set the new course at midnight, and went to his cabin. He left the ship's third mate in charge. He told him to steer back into the normal shipping lane in a few minutes, when the danger was past. However, he didn't tell him the ship was on **autopilot**.

The wreck of the *Exxon Valdez* with support ships.

The third mate changed the course back to the shipping lane, or so he thought. Eleven minutes passed. The giant ship plunged on into the darkness. Unknown to the third mate it was heading on the wrong course. Suddenly the rocks of Bligh Reef loomed up on the **radar**. But by now it was too late. The *Exxon Valdez* ploughed into the reef, punching eight gaping holes in the tanker's **starboard** side. Two of its 13 giant tanks were punctured. Then it smashed on into the main Bligh Reef. Six more tanks were gashed open and oil spilled from its ruptured tanks. The *Exxon Valdez* had struck disaster.

This is the story of the disaster as witnessed by James Kunkel, chief mate of the *Exxon Valdez*.

I feared for my life. I wondered if we were going to see the sunrise.

*There was so much **hull** damage. The reef below was being ground to tiny pieces. The ship was unstable. It could have come off the rocks at any time.*

It still had more than 42 million gallons [190 million litres] of oil on board, and we didn't want to spill any more. It was in danger of sinking. We would have been drowned.

A poison slick

For sea life oil is a kind of poison. When birds try to clean oil from their feathers, they swallow large amounts of it. The fur of seals and otters becomes clogged with oil. When this happens it means that they cannot float or keep warm. They sink and die. The 150-km oil slick from the *Exxon Valdez* proved to be deadly. The slick **contaminated** 2000 km of coastline. Wherever the oil touched the shore the sea **environment** began to die.

The Clear-Up Begins

As the *Exxon Valdez* lay stranded on rocks, emergency action should have begun. But for 12 hours nothing happened. The ship's owners and the local government couldn't agree on what to do. As people talked, the weather turned bad. Storms churned the **oil slick** into a thick sludge, which washed out into the sea.

The *Exxon Valdez* did not sink. No-one died. Yet the oil slick quickly became an **environmental** disaster. Cleaning up after the *Exxon Valdez* disaster took many months. 10,000 people were involved, and it cost $2.5 billion. No-one knew whether the seas and beaches could ever fully recover.

1 Eleven minutes after midnight, disaster strikes. The *Exxon Valdez* ploughs into rocks on Bligh **Reef**. The captain is in his cabin, and has been drinking. He was later sacked for breaking the company's rules.

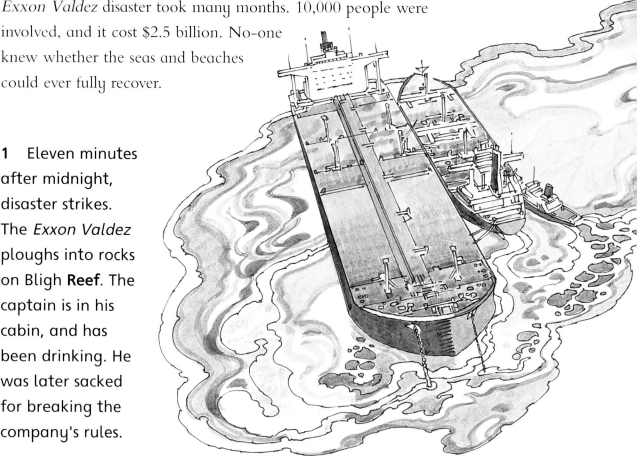

2 Oil is pumped from the damaged ship into rescue tankers. But workers can't pump it out quickly enough – it is spilling into the sea at a rate of 200,000 gallons (910,000 litres) a minute. Storms push the oil slick out into Prince William Sound.

5 Birds and animals are caught in the thick sludge of oil. Hundreds of thousands begin to die. The fishing industry has to stop work.

4 Clean-up teams work with local **volunteers** to mop up the tide of oil. Boats tow booms to skim the oil off the sea. On the beaches hoses and chemicals, and huge mechanical sponges are used to clean rocks. But on the next tide, there is more oil brought in by the sea. The slick washes over 2000km of coastline.

3 It is 36 hours before a floating **boom** is placed around the ship to stop oil spreading. By now it is too late to hold the oil back. Bad weather means the only way to clean up the oil slick is to scoop it from the sea. Most of it will be impossible to clean up. Equipment stored for just such an emergency is under deep snow. Half of it does not work.

The Cost of Disaster

Scientists are still arguing about how much damage the *Exxon Valdez* disaster really did. The spill killed hundreds of thousands of fish, sea-birds and otters. Scientists working for the oil company that owned the ship say that the **environment** has not been damaged for ever. The numbers of birds in the area are now the same as before the disaster. Fish such as salmon seem to live and breed without problems.

Other scientists are not convinced that the animal and plant life of Prince William Sound has recovered. Birds like the murre, a small bird which is a bit like a penguin, no longer breed. They have also found baby salmon that are hatching malformed or even dead.

Scientists found that cleaning up the oil also did a lot of damage. The hot water hoses and chemicals used to clean the oil from beaches killed important sea plants, and actually made the beaches worse in some cases.

Super bugs that eat oil

Tiny bugs – or **bacteria** – live everywhere. Each type of bacteria has a favourite food. For instance, some bacteria cause the mould that grows on old food, or on damp bathroom walls. There are even bacteria that like to eat oil!

After the *Exxon Valdez* disaster special bacteria were sprayed on patches of oil-covered beach. The tests showed that these little bacteria could actually eat the spilled oil that was so poisonous to sea life. In just five months they could leave beaches almost clean. These bacteria are now being used to help clean up after many oil spills.

The clean-up operation on the coastline of Alaska following the *Exxon Valdez* disaster. Hot water hoses were used to remove the oil.

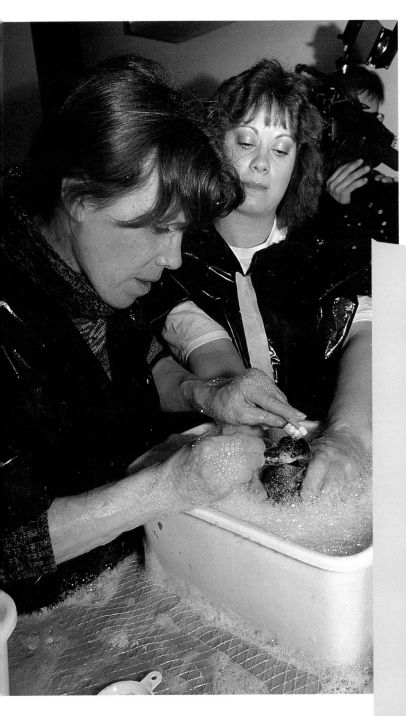

An oil-covered sea-bird, one of the many victims of the Exxon Valdez oil spill, is being carefully cleaned using an old toothbrush.

Disaster brings new laws

The *Exxon Valdez* disaster, and public reaction to it, meant that the US government was forced to take action. It passed the Oil **Pollution** Act in 1990. This law put tougher penalties on companies responsible for oil spills. Tanker owners and oil companies must now make emergency plans in case of accidents. All tankers using US waters are required to have double **hulls**, so there is less chance they will sink or leak oil. A special 'spill fund' has also been set up – paid for by a tax on each barrel of oil. People in areas affected by oil spills can claim money from this fund.

Oil War!
The Gulf War Oil Spills

In the months of January and February 1991, as war raged across the deserts of Kuwait and Iraq, retreating soldiers began a campaign of **sabotage**. They blew up hundreds of **oil wells** and began emptying oil into the sea. It threatened to be one of the worst **environmental** disasters the world had ever seen.

When the sky turned black

The Gulf War began because Iraq had **invaded** Kuwait. Kuwait had some of the largest **oil fields** in the world. Iraq wanted control over this oil. American and European soldiers attacked the Iraqi army and forced them to retreat. But as Iraq's army left Kuwait, its soldiers did as much damage as possible.

Moving through the oil fields, they began by blowing up oil wells. By the end of February 1991 over 730 oil wells were turned into towers of flame. Thick oily smoke shot into the air, turning the skies of Kuwait black with **toxic** smoke. The plume of smoke climbed up to over 4 km high. Experts predicted that the fires could burn for years.

The burning oil wells blocked out the sun and turned the day as cold as night.

A seemingly endless flow of oil gushes from sabotaged and war-damaged oil pipes.

Iraqi soldiers also dumped oil from tankers and stores on the coast. Other oil spewed from war-damaged **storage tanks** and oil pipelines bombed by US and European forces. A massive **oil slick** formed, and spread slowly across the clear blue waters of the Persian Gulf. Over 6 million barrels of oil spilled into the sea. The slick, covering 960 square km of sea, moved slowly south. It covered beaches and rocks, killing birds, fish and sea life.

Hammad Butti, an oil worker from Kuwait, saw and heard the sabotage that was to cause so much damage. This interview appeared in the *National Geographic* magazine in August 1991.

On Sunday 17 February, they began to fire the wells. They put dynamite in each, put a sandbag on each **charge** *to direct the blast downward and* **detonated** *it with an electric charge. Every 10 or 15 minutes they fired another well – boom! Soon the sky was full of fire and smoke.*

21

The Legacy of a War

At the end of the Gulf War much of Kuwait was in ruins. Over 100,000 soldiers and **civilians** from all sides had been killed. Lakes of oil covered miles of Kuwaiti desert. Dynamited **oil wells** burned fiercely. The capital city was ghostly quiet and dark under a blanket of thick black smoke.

1   In August 1990 Kuwait is **invaded** and occupied by Iraq. In January and February 1991 Iraqi troops are forced to retreat. Soldiers begin to **sabotage** Kuwait's oil industry, blowing up oil wells and dumping stored oil into the sea.

2   The huge Mina al-Ahmadi oil **refinery** is emptied. Between 6 and 8 million barrels of oil flood into the Persian Gulf. There is massive **pollution**. An **oil slick** floats south with the currents, covering 480km of beaches. Between 1 and 2 million birds are killed by the oil. Fish and sea animals die. Delicate corals and coastal plants like mangrove trees are devastated.

3   By February 1991 732 oil wells burn out of control. Some fires shoot 60m into the air. The smoke and pollution drift 2400km into northern India, where the oil blackens the snow. Other destroyed wells do not catch fire but gush oil, forming poisonous black lakes, some more than 1.5km long.

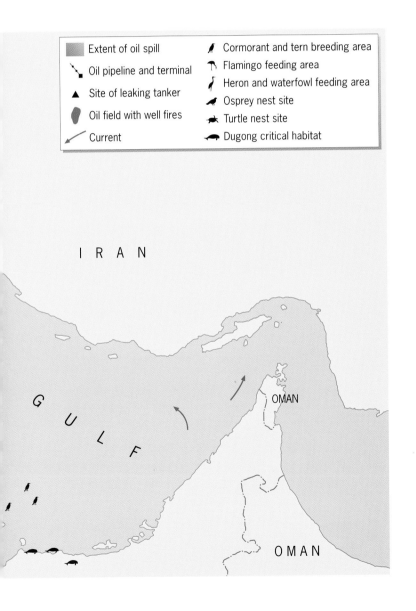

Extent of oil spill	Cormorant and tern breeding area
Oil pipeline and terminal	Flamingo feeding area
Site of leaking tanker	Heron and waterfowl feeding area
Oil field with well fires	Osprey nest site
Current	Turtle nest site
	Dugong critical habitat

IRAN

GULF

OMAN

OMAN

4   It takes till November to **cap** the last burning oil well. Then the clean-up begins. Oil is scraped from beaches and bays. Around 1.4 million barrels of oil are collected and dumped in pits. The job is made more difficult and dangerous by the **land-mines** and bombs left from the war.

Damaged Seas

An **environmental** study six months after the disaster in the Gulf said the effects had been 'tragic'. But the study also said it could have been worse. Another study, by the International Atomic Energy Agency's marine experts, was carried out from June to October 1991. They found that 'severe oil **pollution** was restricted to the Saudi Arabian coastline within about 400km of the spillages'.

Marine experts also said that they had found less pollution than normal in some areas of the Gulf. This was because the war had stopped the normal trade in oil which spills around 2 million barrels of oil into the Persian Gulf every year.

Oil workers struggle to cap a gushing oil well in Kuwait.

However, there is no doubt that the oil spills hurt Kuwait badly. On some beaches oil and sand mixed to form a surface like road tarmac 30cm thick. Oil experts also worked out that it takes the Persian Gulf at least five years to flush out polluted water through the narrow channel that connects it to the world's oceans. Many experts say it will take many years to heal the damage.

Stopping the fires

Stopping – or **capping** – an **oil well** is dangerous work. Once the fire is out, a giant plug has to be jammed into the well, and mud pumped in to stop the well for good. In Kuwait there was the added danger of **land-mines** left from the war. Mines often had to be cleared before fire-fighters and oil well experts could start work.

Wildlife in danger

The Persian Gulf teems with sea life. Its shallow, warm waters are a perfect home for shrimps, oysters and coral. There are turtles, flamingos and the dugong, a large gentle mammal. The rare dugong was one of the animals most at risk in the oil spill. Even before the Gulf War it was thought the dugong might have been wiped out by oil pollution. The oil disaster in the Gulf has made its fight for survival even more difficult.

Dugongs, or manatees, were at great risk from the oil pollution.

Oil and Safety

Most disasters don't have to happen. The Disaster Prevention Unit at Bradford University in the UK has studied over 1000 disasters. It showed that six in every ten could have been avoided. This is true for the oil disasters in this book. Perhaps only the Gulf War disaster was difficult to prevent. If an army decides to **sabotage** an **oil field**, it is very hard to stop them.

A Piper Alpha survivor can at last go home. Many others lost their lives, but important lessons were learnt from the disaster.

Alternatively, the Piper Alpha disaster showed that important safety lessons should have already been learnt from other North Sea accidents. For instance, experts had already agreed that it was not a good idea to have men living over a part of an **oil rig** which could explode. If only Piper Alpha had been built differently, many lives could have been saved.

In the *Exxon Valdez* disaster better emergency equipment would have stopped much of the oil spill from spreading. If people in charge had acted quickly, the giant **oil slick** might never have washed out into the sea.

The reason why safety precautions are not taken is often to do with money. People in the oil industry have to make a profit to stay in business. They do not want to spend money until they know safety measures are going work. We are also to blame, because we do not want things to cost more. And more safety means more cost. How much more would we be willing to pay for oil and all the things that come from it, such as heating or car travel?

A history of oil

People have known about oil for thousands of years. They burnt it for light, and used it for waterproofing. In the 1850s kerosene was distilled for the first time from oil and used as cheap fuel for lamps.

The first **oil wells** were sunk in Germany in 1857. The first American oil well was sunk in Pennsylvania in 1859. When the petrol engine was invented, and cars became more common after the First World War, the oil industry became an essential part of the modern world.

In 1905, as oil became big business, oil **derricks** were built all over what had been a residential area of Los Angeles.

The World's Worst Oil Disasters

Torrey Canyon, UK, 18 March 1967 An oil tanker hits rocks off Cornwall. 120,000 tonnes of oil wash into the sea.

Amoco Cadiz, France, March 1978 An oil tanker breaks up off the French coast and spills 220,000 tonnes of oil.

Ixtoc oil rig, Mexico, 3 June 1979 An oil rig blow-out in the Gulf of Mexico. 500,000 tonnes of oil **pollute** the sea.

Atlantic Empress and *Aegean Captain*, Caribbean Sea, 19 July 1979 Two tankers collide and spill 280,000 tonnes of oil.

Piper Alpha, UK, 6 July 1988 Oil and gas explode on an oil rig. 167 people are killed. The rig is destroyed.

Exxon Valdez, USA, 25 March 1989 An oil tanker hits rocks off the Alaskan coast. 30,000 tonnes of oil wash into the sea.

Gulf War, January-November 1991 Oil **well** and oil storage **sabotage** spills 6 to 8 million barrels of oil and destroys over 730 oil wells.

Fergana Valley, Uzbekistan, March 1992 An oil well blow-out spills over 6 million barrels of oil onto the land around the well. The blow-out lasts 62 days.

The world's oil

On this map of the world the main oil-producing countries are marked. You can also see where the world's worst oil disasters and pollution are.

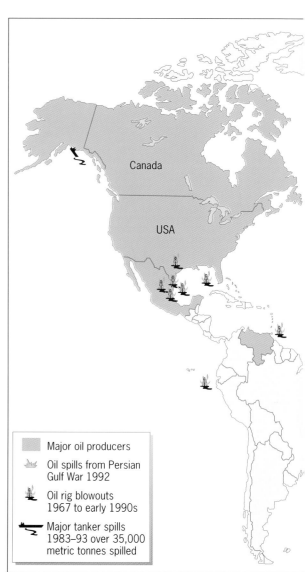

Canada

USA

Major oil producers

Oil spills from Persian Gulf War 1992

Oil rig blowouts 1967 to early 1990s

Major tanker spills 1983–93 over 35,000 metric tonnes spilled

Oil wells ablaze in Libya. Oil is an important industry in the Middle East.

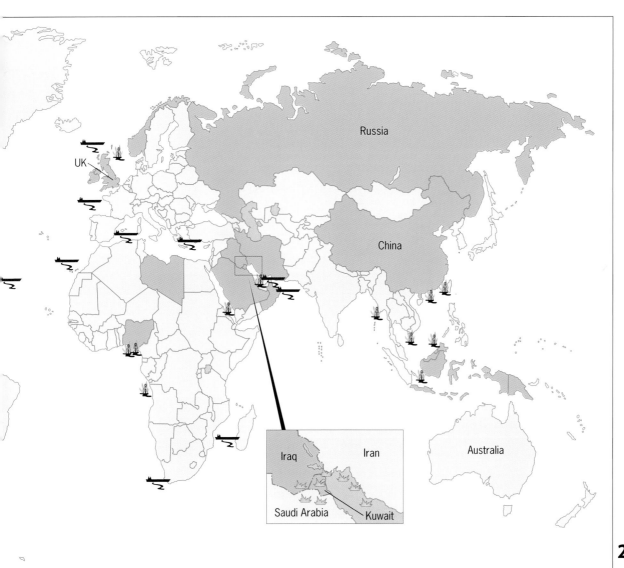

Glossary

autopilot automatic pilot, allowing a plane or ship to steer itself

bacteria simplest and smallest form of plant life. They live in large numbers in the air, soil and water.

boom floating barrier used to stop oil slicks spreading

cap/capping to stop up an oil well

civilian non-military person; someone not in the armed services (army, air force, navy etc)

charge small quantity of explosive

contaminated something which has a dangerous substance on or in it

derrick the framework to hold the drilling machinery over an oil well

detonated when something is blown up

environment/environmental external surroundings: the land, water and air around us. Environment can also refer to a particular place, such as the sea.

evacuate move people from a dangerous place

explosive substance that can explode/something that is liable to explode

fertilizer food for plants used by farmers and gardeners on their crops and plants

flare signal light used at sea, usually as a sign of distress

hull body of a boat or ship

ignite set on fire

invade enter a country by military force, usually with the aim of taking control of that country

land-mine explosive mine (bomb) laid on or under the ground

oil field place where there is a lot of oil underground

oil rig metal structure in the middle of the sea used to drill out oil from deep below the seabed. The bit above the water is called a platform. It is held up by long legs that are buried in the seabed.

oil slick smooth patch of oil on the sea

oil well a deep bore hole drilled down into the ground to get to oil

pesticides chemicals used to kill or control insects on plants

pollution poisonous or harmful substances that can damage the environment

preservative something added to food to make it stay fresh longer

pressure force of one thing in contact with another, in this case of air inside a container

radar way of detecting objects using radio waves

reef ridge of rock just under the surface of the sea

refining separating oil into its many different parts, such as petrol, tar and gas

refinery place where oil is refined

sabotage damage something on purpose

SOS international code of extreme distress. Also called Mayday.

starboard right-hand side of a boat or ship

storage tank large tank used to hold oil or other liquids

supertanker a giant and fast ship which can carry a huge cargo

toxic poisonous

union organization which represents groups of workers

valve tap inside a pipe which can be turned off or on

volunteer person who gives up their time to help (without being paid)

Index